Look What I

Can Do Now

For More Booklets...

Interested in more copies of *Look What I Can Do Now* to share with others? Each of the booklets in the *Me, Too!* series is available in packages of five.

Looking for guidance on every aspect of developing inclusive preschool strategies? The complete set of all six booklets in the *Me, Too!* series will provide you with extensive techniques for enhancing children's early years.

Contact Brookes Publishing Co. at *410-337-9580* or *1-800-638-3775,* or visit our web site at *www.brookespublishing.com.*

To write to the publisher: Paul H. Brookes Publishing Co., Post Office Box 10624, Baltimore, Maryland 21285-0624, U.S.A.

Typeset by Integrated Publishing Solutions, Grand Rapids, Michigan.
Manufactured in the United States of America by H & N Printing & Graphics, Timonium, Maryland.
Cover art and interior illustrations by Lori Esposito.

The *Me, Too!* series is based on research conducted through the Early Childhood Research Institute on Inclusion supported by Grant #HO242K4004 from the U.S. Department of Education, Office of Special Education Programs. No official endorsement by the federal government should be inferred.

Parent quotes and case scenarios are from actual people and events. In all instances, names have been changed; in some instances, identifying details have been altered to protect confidentiality.

Library of Congress Cataloging-in-Publication Data

Hanson, Marci J.
Look what I can do now / [Marci J. Hanson and Maria L. Morgan].
p. cm. — (Me, too!)
ISBN 1-55766-514-1
1. Handicapped children—Services for. 2. Preschool children—Services for. 3. Architecture and handicapped children. 4. Architecture and the physically handicapped. 5. Parents of handicapped children—Handbooks, manuals, etc. I. Morgan, Maria L. II. Title. III. Series.
HV888 .H367 2001
649′.15—dc21 00-068080

British Library Cataloguing in Publication data are available from the British Library.

Baltimore • London • Toronto • Sydney

Introduction

Chances are, if you're reading this booklet, you have a child between the ages of 2 and 5 years. It's a time of new experiences and challenges for children and their parents. As a parent, you are accustomed to making decisions to help your child grow, develop, and learn in appropriate ways, but now, you will also be deciding how to help your child belong and participate in school and other community activities. Will your child make friends? Will your child know how to behave? Will your child be able to do the things the other children are doing?

This booklet is one in a series called *Me, Too!*, designed particularly for families of young children with disabilities. Although these booklets are written directly to parents and other family members, teachers, child care providers, and other professionals will find them valuable, too. Plan to pass these booklets back and forth among the adults who are important in your child's life. Here is a brief description of each booklet:

Introducing Me: This booklet is different from the other booklets because it is one that you create. You fill out the pages to tell others about your child. Share this booklet with your child's teachers and with the other professionals and caregivers who work with your child.

It's Time for Preschool: This booklet helps you learn more about selecting a preschool for your child, connecting with teachers and other families, knowing what the law guarantees you, and making the early school years a positive experience for your child.

My Community, My Family: This booklet helps you learn about building good relationships between your family and others in the community. You will find good advice on locating appropriate, accessible programs and activities. Strategies also are included for making activities meet the needs of all children.

My New Friends: This booklet explores ways that you can encourage friendships between children. The importance of friendships is highlighted through suggestions designed to help your child develop friendships with classmates and make new friends in the community.

On My Best Behavior: This booklet will help you understand your child's behavior. You will learn techniques to help you support positive behavior, discourage negative behavior, and avoid behavior problems by planning ahead for new situations.

Look What I Can Do Now: This booklet focuses on introducing strategies for modifying schedules and the physical environment to make it easier for your child to participate in programs and activities.

In each of these booklets, we will be talking about the term *inclusion*. Inclusion usually refers to the joint participation of children with and without disabilities in school and community programs and in activities. Although people may think of inclusion as something that only happens at school, inclusion is actually a very broad concept that refers to participation in many settings (e.g., child care, recreational programs, libraries, religious activities, athletic organizations, museums). In the most general sense, inclusion is about belonging. When a child belongs, he or she is a part of a group and has opportunities to join activities with other children. Inclusion is good for children.

We hope that the *Me, Too!* series will help you as you begin to develop inclusive strategies to meet your family's needs. You will find experiences and recommendations that other parents have shared with us to help you. We address issues and decisions commonly faced by parents and suggest strategies for you to consider when planning for your child and family. As you study these ideas, always keep in mind that you, as a parent, are the expert as to what works for your family!

Look What I Can Do Now

When you take your child to preschool, a special activity, or a community event, do you ever feel apprehensive about how well your child will be able to participate with other children? Do you worry that the room seems too crowded and that your child won't be able to move around easily? Does it seem that the group moves from one activity to another more quickly than is comfortable for your child? At home, does your child sometimes wander and have a difficult time finding something to do? When you go to the park, does your child seem to have nothing to do because of her disability? Do you wonder what you can do to help your child? In these situations, parents, teachers, and others concerned about children can meet to discuss adaptations that will help children at home and in the community. By planning specific adaptations, you can make sure that your child gets the most of these early years and is better able to enjoy the time he spends at preschool and in the community.

Basically, adaptations are any changes that you make to support children as they participate in activities. Many situations and materials can be adapted for your child. Changes to toys, books, equipment, ways of teaching, and ways of communicating help your child enjoy the same experiences as his peers. Adaptations are designed to help children play with others, play with toys, look at books, understand others, make new friends, and learn new things. Look for the bubbles icon for special tips.

MAKING ADAPTATIONS

More often than not, you, the parent, will be the first person to notice that your child needs certain adaptations. Your child's teachers or care providers also may be able to suggest adaptations that will help your child learn and participate. When parents and other caregivers notice challenges or have ideas about changes that can be made, they can meet as a team to discuss necessary adaptations and how to make them. Creative, appropriate adaptations are more easily developed and used when your child's entire team—parents, teachers, therapists, aides, administrators, and others—is involved in planning and problem solving.

Because your child's teachers or child care providers may have made similar adaptations for other children in the past or may know of simple ways to accommodate your child's needs, enlisting their help can be very effective. If your child has an individualized education program (IEP), it should list your child's instructional and support goals and the people responsible for each goal so that all members of the team are aware of changes that need to be made. Many of the members of your child's IEP team have the background and training to suggest and help make any adaptations that your child may need. If you feel that your child could benefit from adaptations, begin by making a list of her activities at home, at school, and in the community. Identify the types of changes that are needed by asking yourself questions:

- Does my child need more time to get from one activity to the next?
- Does my child need more time to complete activities?
- Does my child have trouble navigating the classroom because things are in the way?
- Does my child have trouble getting around the playground or park because of the terrain?
- Does my child have trouble playing with certain toys? Is it because of physical trouble with the toy or difficulty understanding how to use the toy?

- Does my child have trouble understanding or joining in a group activity? What about the activity seems to be difficult?
- Does my child need to receive more adult help with certain activities?
- Does my child seem unable to get involved in group activities or games?

OPPORTUNITIES FOR ADAPTATIONS

If you answered "yes" to one or more of these questions, you probably have already started thinking about possible adaptations for your child. Because young children are learning in virtually every setting, during many different daily routines and activities, you may be overwhelmed by the number of adaptations that you feel should be made. Begin by changing the daily routines and activities in which everyone participates and adapting the materials and equipment that everyone uses. Even minor adaptations at home, at school, and in the community can help your child participate. As your child becomes accustomed to the changes you have made, you can continue to make more adaptations. The easiest place to begin making adaptations is at home. Family routines and activities that can be adapted include

- Getting up in the morning
- Going on family errands
- Snack and meal times
- Playing with pets
- Gardening or other yard work
- Riding in the car, on the bus, or on the train
- Playing outside
- Helping clean up around the home
- Playing with brothers and sisters
- Staying with a baby sitter

- Bath time
- Story time
- Getting ready for bed

Because many children spend a portion of each day at preschool and child care programs, it is a good idea to think about the types of activities that may need to be adapted for your child in these settings. Typical preschool routines and activities include

- Arriving and stowing personal belongings
- Saying hello
- Circle time
- Arts and crafts activities
- Small-group activities
- Indoor play activities
- Clean-up
- Snack or meal time
- Rest or quiet time
- Outdoor play activities
- Gathering belongings for dismissal
- Getting ready to go home
- Saying good-bye

Interaction with different members of your community helps your child develop important social skills and encourages others to get to know your child. The community offers many activities, such as the following, for you and your child to enjoy and additional opportunities to make successful adaptations for your child:

- Religious activities
- Doctor's office visits

- Riding the bus or subway and carpooling
- Karate, dance, swim, or YMCA-type classes
- Parks and recreational athletics
- Grocery shopping
- Playing at the park
- Birthday parties

It is also a good idea to call ahead and ask if specific programs or activities can be adapted for your child. During some activities, such as birthday parties, the person in charge may feel more comfortable if you remain with your child. Again, checking in advance can make a situation more comfortable for everyone.

"He can't walk in his walker in the classroom. The teacher called me and said they're going to try and arrange the furniture to where he can handle the space. And I'm going up there tomorrow to see what she's done."

—Nicholas' mother

CREATIVE SOLUTIONS

Let's look at some specific examples of common adaptations and at supports that you may be able to modify for your child's needs. You'll find general tips for a broad range of situations as well as some specific examples. You can try these ideas at home, at preschool, at child care, during dance or swim class, or during library storytime, and you can use your creativity to adapt them for other settings.

Read through these examples, and choose the suggestions that you think will be useful for your child. The tips are divided into several categories to help you identify different changes that will help your child fully participate at home, in school, and in the community. Have fun!

Communication

To help your child learn and understand, you may have to change the way you, and others who regularly interact with your child, are accustomed to communicating. Altering facial expressions and your speaking pace will help you capture your child's attention and keep her interest in an activity.

Pause when you talk or play with children to encourage them to request, respond, or answer. As you talk with your child about the people and things he sees at the grocery store, pause occasionally to give your child an opportunity to point to or name an item or object. When your child is excited about something he sees, look expectantly at him and wait for him to talk or point. Keep your child interested in being at the grocery store by involving him in your selections—give him choices about what to purchase. Hold up two objects, name each one for him, and pause to encourage him to choose one.

Exaggerate facial expressions and use interesting intonation patterns to get children's attention and keep their interest. When we talk to infants, small children, and pets, we tend to use playful, fun, or exaggerated voices. Children pick up on these changes in tone and learn how parents sound when they are angry, sad, happy, or excited. Show happiness, surprise, or excitement in your voice and with your expression as you play Chase with the dog, pet the gerbil, or roll a ball to the cat. These signals can alert your child to exciting and interesting activities. She may pay attention to what you're doing and even want to join the fun when she hears your animation.

Use a slower pace of speaking and moving or gesturing to allow children time to notice and respond to cues. At dance, swim, or karate class, speak to children slowly, and pause between phrases or short sentences to give them time to follow what you are saying. As you speak, use gestures that match the words you are saying. For example, when telling children to jump, demonstrate the action by using your whole body or by using hand movements. Try to use the same word or phrases to express yourself so your child can become familiar with language that refers to specific items or actions. Clearly enunciating will help your child learn proper pronunciation and word usage as well.

Notes for other adaptations to communication methods:

The Physical Space

Adaptations to the physical settings of our environment are quite common: You may choose to have the books that you use most on a shelf close to your desk or workspace. Just as a chef organizes spices, knives, and mixing bowls according to his needs, children benefit from adaptations to physical space. Many adaptations are made without any conscious planning during regular daily routines. Frequently used toys are stored in places easily accessible to children, and hazardous materials are kept where children can't reach them. Some children, though, require more deliberate adaptations to the physical spaces that they encounter every day. These changes in physical settings help children join in activities and learn.

Change the arrangement of the furniture to contribute to easier movement throughout the room. At a child care center, observe the room to spot potential barriers. Do any pieces of furniture, tables, chairs, shelves, or toys prevent children from easily moving from one area to another? Also, look for any obstacles that prevent children from easily seeing people and toys in other areas. Change the arrangement of the furniture in the room so all children can see what is happening in other areas and can easily access all parts of the room.

Make the playground accessible to all children. Watch your child play at the park or playground. Can he move himself independently from one area to another? Can he safely ride on the swings or the teeter-totter or go down the slide? Think about the toys and equipment that your child cannot use at the park and which changes are needed so he *can* use them. For example, removing wood chips from a path to create a smooth, packed dirt surface makes it possible for children to walk or use a wheelchair to move themselves without getting stuck. Ground or protective cover that provides some padding, such as the padding that encircles ice skating rinks, may protect children from injury should they fall. Replacing a swing with one that provides more support allows children to swing without falling. Making the sides of a slide taller helps children go down the slide more safely. Discuss these adaptations with your child's teacher or care provider and the site supervisor. If the program doesn't attempt to respond to your concerns, you can work with your local family resource center on disability advocacy to help achieve access for your child.

Arrange the materials to encourage communication and social interaction. During bath time, put one or two of your child's favorite bath toys in the water. Place other favorites in a nearby tub or net. Your child may notice the other toys and ask for one or more of them by pointing, gesturing, looking at the toys, or using words to ask for your help to get them. You could also give your child a few of the toys she likes to play with at bath time and then wait to see if she asks for the rest. For example, if she likes to put animals in a boat, give her the boat and one animal, and wait for her signal that she wants the other animals, too.

Make the physical setting safe for all children. In community settings, such as Sunday school or the public library, try moving around the room at a child's-eye view. Put any heavy objects you notice up where children can't get to them. Children enjoy investigating their surroundings and are likely to explore anything within their reach—a heavy bookend may look interesting to a child until he drops it on his foot! Objects small enough to fit into your child's mouth should

also be kept out of reach. If you can't move a potentially hazardous object, you can make it safe by altering or securing it. Try padding or rounding the sharp corners of furniture. To keep toys and other materials safe and clean, laminate books or toys so they can easily be washed with an anti-bacterial soap.

Arrange materials so an area is inviting to multiple children. At a birthday party, create opportunities for interaction and play by setting chairs or pillows around tables or play areas so that two or more children can sit together. Try to provide duplicates of popular or favorite toys and party favors in case children want to play with the same toy. Activities that involve toys such as dishes and dolls, houses with cars and people, or interesting blocks with cars to knock them down encourage two or more children to play with one another.

Notes for making changes to physical space:

Playing with Playmates

Social interaction during the preschool years is important because it lays the groundwork for the ways in which children will relate to one another from youth to adulthood. Encouraging interactions between children with and without disabilities allows them to begin developing opinions and friendships based on their own contacts and experiences.

Play games that all children find interesting and that allow two or more children to participate. During the preschool years, many games and activities provide children with physical exercise. They also create opportunities to form friendships and learn values such as sharing, helping, and healthy competition. At their child care center, encourage children to engage in activities that they enjoy and that include two or more participants. Some activities that appeal to preschoolers include

- Tug-of-war (using thick ropes or blankets)
- Pushing or swinging in a swing
- Pulling or riding in a wagon
- Giving a ride on the back of a tricycle
- Pushing toy cars back and forth to another child
- Throwing and/or catching a ball
- Building a tower of blocks and knocking it over
- Playing house

Help and encourage children as they begin to play together. For example, comment on what each child is doing, and suggest what might happen next. Give children physical assistance as needed to participate in the play. As children need less support, remove yourself from the activity, but remain nearby to provide help and supervision.

Encourage children to develop a variety of different play partners. Because children with and without disabilities may not initially play together on their own, help them approach new playmates by showing and telling children how to ask each other to play. At the park or playground, help a child ask a classmate or neighbor to swing next to her, to play ball, or to ride on the teeter-totter. Show the children how to communicate with each other, demonstrating the words to use and methods to get each other's attention. Show the children how to make eye contact and get at each other's eye level. Share words that the child with a disability will understand. Show children how to hold a toy so others can see it and how to point to toys and people to help others understand.

Notes for playing with playmates:

Learning from Playmates

Adults often overlook the importance of children to each other. How many times have you heard a parent say, "Oh, that's just something she picked up at school?" Parents, teachers, and care providers are a great influence on young children, but children often learn a lot just from being with their peers. When young children interact, they learn important social skills such as humility, responsibility, compassion, communication, and helpfulness. For good or bad, they also learn new habits, words, interests, and games from one another. Because children are such strong influences on each other, peers and classmates can model what to do or say and encourage children with disabilities as they learn.

Help children to help others by demonstrating what to do or say during an activity. Create opportunities for children to be a "buddy" to a child with a disability in community activities. Show the buddy how to help the child by holding hands to go to a new activity or giving the child a toy or a turn when playing a game. Teach children songs, rhymes, or special games to play together; then, have them reinforce what they have learned by playing with one another.

Help children to help each other by providing assistance during an activity. At preschool, encourage children who have mastered skills to demonstrate those skills to children who have not. Actions and expressions that one child can demonstrate for another include

- Greeting others during arrival and departure routines
- Asking and answering questions during circle time
- Using expressions of courtesy such as "Please" and "Thank you"
- Asking for and sharing toys or materials
- Asking permission to do something

After one child models greeting another person, answering a question about a picture or story, or choosing a color when making an art project, ask the child with a disability to do or say the same thing.

Help motivate a child to participate in an activity by asking the other children to praise and encourage the child as they help with the activity. Encourage brothers and sisters to use words and gestures that motivate and reinforce their sibling. For example, giving a high-five for building a tower of blocks together or saying, "You can do it!" as the child is learning to climb the stairs to the top of a slide can help motivate the child with a disability to participate in the activity.

Notes for learning from playmates:

Adapted Materials

Adaptations to materials used on a daily basis help make it easier for children to make choices and use the materials without additional support. Although adapting physical spaces or activities encourages participation, changes in materials allow a child to use them as independently as possible. You can change activity rules, make toys safer, or secure furniture for additional stability to enable the participation of all children.

Store materials at an appropriate height for children, and ensure that materials are appropriately designed to encourage children to be more independent. In community settings, such as churches or activity centers, help children reach toys and materials that are usually on inaccessible shelves or countertops by moving the toys to lower shelves. Help a child paint or draw at an easel by lowering the easel and providing a child-sized chair to sit on while at the easel. You can also buy or make a tabletop easel so your child can sit at the table to paint or draw. You may want to discuss these changes with the program staff to help them discover ways of making it possible for each child to participate.

Use tape, Velcro, and nonskid backing to help hold materials in place as children use them. If your child's arm movements cause paper to slide off the table, ask the teacher to attach the paper to the table with masking tape. If your child has trouble holding toys or if they sometimes fall over when he tries to use them, use clamps or Velcro to attach toys to a hard surface. Attach a section of a bath mat or bathtub appliqués to the seats of chairs if children seem to slip and slide when they sit.

Allow children to join traditional activities in different ways. "Circle time" songs and rhymes at preschool may involve bodily movements that some children have not yet mastered. A child who is not yet walking will not be able to participate fully with a group singing "Ring Around the Rosie." Change the game so that children crawl rather than walk. You could also suggest that all of the children sit in a circle, hold hands, and rock side to side.

Make the materials larger or brighter. If your child cannot grasp the small handles of a shovel and pail when playing in a sand box, wrap foam and tape around the handles to make them larger. To help your child see and use sand toys, put colorful tape around the edge of the pail and a different bright color around the edge of the shovel.

Notes for using other adapted materials:

Child Preferences

Whereas adaptations to activities, materials, and spaces often stimulate children and motivate them to participate, sometimes simply using a favorite toy, activity, or person will help get children's attention and keep them interested. Familiar or favorite settings, people, and objects are calming during times of stress or adjustment. It is often helpful to use something familiar or preferred when introducing children to new material and situations.

Let your child hold favorite quiet toys to help pacify her. Because your child may have difficulty riding in the car or on the bus, she may want to get out or may have tantrums during the trip. To keep your child

relaxed and interested in being in the car or on the bus, have several favorite quiet toys available and let her play with one or more of them.

Help make successful transitions from one activity to the next by letting your child play with his favorite toy or friend. Try moving a favorite toy or person and see if your child follows. When your child has difficulty staying in bed at bedtime, place a favorite quiet toy, such as a doll, teddy bear, or blanket, in the bed. Bedtime rituals such as reading a favorite book or story, saying prayers, or putting toys and stuffed animals "to sleep" can also signal transition and produce a calming effect.

Notes for using child preferences:

Simplified Activities

Just as most adult daily routines are too complicated for young children, many school activities can be confusing or frustrating for some children. You can make a task simpler by breaking it into smaller parts or reducing the number of steps. When each step is explained and demonstrated, the routine becomes more familiar, comfortable, and easier for a child to understand.

Break down the task or activity into smaller, more manageable parts. At dance, swim, or karate class, give directions to your child one step at a time. Have her follow each direction after it is given. You can use photographs or posters that illustrate each step of the activity. Pointing to the picture that demonstrates the step as you describe it will reinforce the separate actions that comprise the activity. You may wish to help your child's teacher or care provider learn which adaptations work best for your child.

Change or reduce the number of required steps for an activity. At your child's preschool, if the soap dispenser is located on the wall behind the sink, it may be impossible or difficult for your child to reach. He may have to stand on tiptoes, use a stool, or reach across and above the sink to use the soap. Change or reduce the number of required steps by using a plastic soap dispenser with a pump top. Place it on the counter near the sink, or attach it to the sink with a suction cup.

Notes for simplifying other activities:

Special Materials and Equipment

Specially designed materials can help a child communicate and interact with other children. For example, homemade, individualized communication books help children build friendships by providing a way to share information about themselves with others. Like adaptations to the environment or to activities, using special or adaptive devices allows your child to participate more fully in activities. Special equipment used for young children includes items such as

- Foam mats, heavy carpet, and padding so children can participate in rough-and-tumble play on the floor with adult supervision
- Enlarged tricycle pedals and adapted seat or a special tricycle
- Communication books with pictures of your child's favorite people and toys, plus everyday routines or events
- A computer to print messages with a mouse and touch screen or other adaptive equipment

Sometimes children need other complex or technology-based adaptations. Your child's teacher or special support person may be able to give you information on different kinds of adaptations that will help your child be more successful at school as well as at home and in the community. These adaptations could include devices to help your child communicate, walk independently, or play. Other adaptations may be designed for safety, such as a special child-size helmet for outdoor or indoor play.

Use special materials and equipment to increase your child's access to materials. Your child may have difficulty using riding toys because she cannot reach the pedals or because she needs support to ride safely. The handle of a wagon or other pull toy may not be big enough to allow her to grasp it and pull. To help your child use and play with these toys, enlarge the pedals on riding toys by taping large blocks to them and replace the seat with a larger one that provides more support. Special tricycles that have been designed for children with disabilities can also be purchased (consult support staff before purchasing toys manufactured with special adaptations). Place large pillows in a wagon, or use triwall (corrugated cardboard often used by physical and occupational therapists) to make the sides of the wagon taller so children can ride safely. Enlarge the handle of a wagon by wrapping foam and tape around the handle so children can hold on better and pull more easily.

Use special materials and equipment to increase your child's ability to participate in activities. To help children communicate with one another, make communication books with each child's favorite things. Include favorite, familiar stories from, for example, religious classes or activities. These books are often helpful both when a child talks with the whole group or a specific friend. Some children may use a special device to help them communicate, such as a communication board with symbols, letters, and frequently used words or phrases. Support staff who specialize in augmentative and alternative communication (AAC) can provide input about a system appropriate for your child.

Notes for using other special materials:

Adult Support

Support children's participation by showing them how to respond and by encouraging them to express their ideas and feelings. Join in your child's activities. Use words and gestures that are motivating and meaningful to your child. Give your child a hug once he has dressed, finished his breakfast, or brushed his teeth. Say "Great!" and "Way to go!" when she shows you a drawing or organizes her toys. Act as a translator for your child; explain her behavior and actions by telling others the feelings and emotions your child is trying to express.

Model or show children what to do or say during an activity or event. On family errands, demonstrate for children how to greet other people. Wave and say "Hi" or "Good-bye" as you arrive at or leave a store. Demonstrate how to ask questions or ask for help and how to point so that others understand what you want. Say "Please" and "Thank you" to encourage children to use these words at appropriate times.

Ask yourself how you can modify the suggestions in this booklet according to your child's specific needs and desires. Just as every child is unique, adaptations will be different for each child. Brainstorming with your child's teachers and support staff will help you decide which adaptations will work best for your child.

Join children's play—be there with them. Imitate your child's actions with toys and also demonstrate new ways of playing with them. If possible, provide duplicates of some toys for a babysitter so your child can do this easily. When your child is playing with brothers and sisters, ask the babysitter to stay close by and help the children notice and talk to one another. When you get home, don't interrupt what your child is doing. Instead, take a few moments to join the activity.

Interpret for children by saying words to express the feelings that they are demonstrating through their behavior or actions. At school or the doctor's office, help others understand your child's feelings, ideas, or desires by describing your child's behavior and actions. As your child uses sounds and movements, say the words to express what your child wants, sees, or feels. For example, when your child looks at you and leans toward you, say, "You want me to hold you." When your child looks at a toy that the doctor is holding, say, "You want the toy," and help her reach to get it.

Notes for providing other adult support:

When Adaptations Don't Work

If you make a change that doesn't seem to be successful, team up with others who know your child and think about why this might be so. Adaptations may not work if the activity itself is a special event for your child—he may be so excited about participating in the activity or being in a new place that he doesn't respond to the adaptation. Adaptations are also often ineffective if the place in which the adaptation is made is unfamiliar. When you adapt an activity in which your child doesn't typically participate, he may not respond to the adaptation because it isn't a familiar routine.

You Can Do It!

When making adaptations, it is important to remember to start by making simple changes to situations and settings that already exist. Change activities in which your child participates on a regular basis. Use simple solutions and ideas—start with the adaptation that is the most obvious and the least different. By starting small, you will be looking for what is most appropriate for your child and will avoid overadapting.